THE ODES OF SHALOMÉ

Ancient Netzari Songs of Extraterrestrial Love

ODES are poetic song lyrics of irregular form meant to express fervent emotion. Odes are for singing.

Shalomé bat Maryah

Jackson H. Snyder II

Second Edition:
October 8, 2009

Dedicated to the one hundred fifty-three.

TABLE OF CONTENTS

About the Odes

THE ODES OF SHALOMÉ is generally known as *The Odes of Solomon*. At least one of the *Odes* is directly attributed to Shalomé, the disciple/sister of Yahshua Messiah, in an early witness.[1] Internal evidence of female authorship includes frequent recitals of the Most High's feminine aspects.[2] Reading evokes the pen of a woman of great faith and spiritual clarity.

Trustworthy contemporary scholars tell us that

(1) The original language of the *Odes* is Aramaic – the language of the Messiah and the sect of the Nazoreans,[3]

(2) The origin of the *Odes* may be Edessa in Adiabene – a sanctuary land for persecuted followers of the Messiah,[4]

(3) There is affinity between the language, sentiment, and theology in the *Odes*, the *Gospel According to John*, and the *Dead Sea Scrolls*,

(4) The *Odes* do not contain Gnostic concepts or New Testament quotations.

(5) Since all the *Odes* end with HalleluYah! and water is mentioned throughout, these songs may have been utilized in the early baptismal liturgies of Nazorean assemblies.

Recent archaeological discoveries point to *The Gospel According to John* as originating in the second half of the first century. The similarities between *John* and the *Odes* indicate they may be contemporaneous compositions arising from the same community.

Let us then assume that *The Odes of Shalomé* constitutes the earliest Nazorean hymnbook. As such, this compilation repositions the *Odes* in their original setting, rewording and reworking them to make their meaning more authentic than existing scholarly or 'churchy' translations.

---

[1] In the *Pistis Sophia*, early 2nd century. Shalomé receives mention in the canonical Mark:16:1.

[2] *Master Yahweh*, also spelled M-a-r-i-a *Mary*.

[3] Nazoreans = followers of Yahshua the Anointed aka 'Jesus Christ.'

[4] According to Eusebius *Eccles. History* and the *Letters of Abgar*.

Shalomé in Scripture

From ***The Gospel of Mark*** 10:46 (lacuna restored from ***Secret Mark***): Then Yahshua came into Yericho. The sister of the young man whom Yahshua cherished was there with his mother and Shalomé, but Yahshua would not receive them.

From ***The Gospel of Mark*** (15:40 – 16:3): There were women looking on from a distance, among whom were Maria Magdala, Maryah the mother of Ya'akov the younger, also the mother of Yahshua and Shalomé; who, when Yahshua was in Galilee, followed him and served him.[5] It was preparation *day*; Yosef of Arimathea, an honest councilor, who was also looking for the Reign of Elohim, went in boldly to Pilatus asking for Yahshua's body. Pilate wondered if Yahshua were already dead. Calling the centurion to him, he inquired if he had been dead any time. Thus learning from the centurion, *Pilatus* gave the corpse to Yosef. Yosef bought linen, took him down, wrapped him in the linen, and laid him in a tomb hewn from rock, and rolled a stone to the door of the tomb. Maria Magdala and Yahshua's mother Maryah saw where he was laid. When the Shabbat had passed, Maria Magdala and Maryah the mother of Ya'aqov and Shalomé bought herbs, so they might gather to anoint him. They came to the tomb early on the first of the week, the sun having risen. They said among themselves, Who will roll the stone away from the door of the tomb for us?

From ***The (Greek) Gospel of the Egyptians***: The Mar said, Eat any herb but the bitter one. For I have come to undo the consequences of greed, birth, and aging. Shalomé said, When will we all know these *things have been undone*? The Mar answered, When the rags of shame have been put underfoot – when two become echad – when maleness and femaleness are no longer clearly perceived. *Then* Shalomé asked, How long will death have power? The Mar answered, As long as women have children. Salome replied, It is a good thing that I haven't had any children![6]

From the ***Gospel of Thomas***: Shalomé asks, Who are you, Mari, that you have taken your place on my bench and eaten from my table? Yahshua replies, I am He Who Is of Echad. Whatever belongs to the Father has been given to me.[7] Shalomé replies, And I, I am your talmid! Yahshua answers, When the talmid is Echad, he will be filled with light; but if he is divided, he will be filled with darkness.

NOTE: According to the Egyptian Gospels (remembering that Yahshua's family had ties in Egypt), there were several female talmidim – gender made little difference among these Nazoreans, and both genders of talmidim were considered as 'he.'

---

5 MarYah = "Master YHWH." Maryah, Maria = common names of a women.

6 Quoted from Clement of Alexandria. As long as children are born, all will die.

7 Echad – John 12:49, 13:3, 17:11; Given to me - John 3:35, 5:22, 10:29, 13:3 *etc.*

The Odes of Shalomé

1. **Crown**

MarYah[8] is on my head like a crown, and I will never be without Him. This crown of truth is plaited upon me; it is rooting Your branches so as to blossom forth in me. This is not like a thirsty crown that does not bloom; for You live on my head, and have bloomed on me. Your fruits are full and ripe; they are bursting forth with Yeshuati.[9] Halleluyah.

Response:

2. **Wreath**[10]

Yah, upon my head, a wreath; I will ever dwell beneath.
Plaited orb of verity, branch'd and blossoming in me.
Not a dry crown nor a dead, but a thriving on my head –
Sprouting grapes, so ripe and rife:
Bleeding Fruit who saves my life.
O, dear Father, may You be ever growing as a tree:
Shooting forth from this poor flesh
Many fruits, diverse and fresh.

On my head, a royal crown; on my body, as a gown;
On my feet for all to see: You are woven over me.
When the earth shakes or the sea threatens to bring harm to me,
I need nevermore contend;
Knowing my life has no end.
O, dear Mother, ever be graciously adorning me;
Nourishing my evergreen
Spirit-fruits, diverse and clean.

---

[8] MarYah = the Aramaic expression of the sacred name YHWH. YAH is its poetic abbreviation; in translation it is, "Sovereign Yahweh." Or "Master Yahweh." MarYah may refer to either the Heavenly Father or Yahshua the Son.

[9] Yeshuati = 'my salvation' or 'my Yahshua' – a double meaning found throughout.

[10] Ode 2 is lost. This Ode is a contemporary resetting of Ode 1. The ***responses*** in this volume have been composed by the publisher.

3. **Favor**

I am putting on my Father's favor for He loves me. His bacharim[11] are with Him; I am dependent upon them. (O, He loves me!) I would not have known how to love MarYah had He not loved me since forever. Who is able to distinguish love, except the one who is loved? I love the Beloved, even I myself love Him, and where His Sabbath rests, there rest I also.

I will be no stranger, because MarYah, the El Shaddai,[12] the Merciful one; He is not jealous over me; for I am yachad in Him.[13] The lover has found the Beloved. I love Him, He who is the Son. So I will become a son. The echad with the Eternal will surely be eternal. Likewise, the one who enjoys Life will live. This is the Ruach of MarYah, who is not false, who teaches the children of humankind to know His ways.[14] Be wise and understanding; and be awakened. Halleluyah.

4. **Space**

No one can distort Your sacred space, Eli; nor can anyone change it or put it somewhere else.[15] The other one has no power against it, because You designed Your refuge even before You made any other special spaces.

The Ancient One will not be distorted by His inferiors. You have given Your heart, O MarYah, to Your Tzadikim.[16] Never will You be idle nor will You be without fruits: For one hour of Your faith excels all days and years.

Who will clothe themselves with Your favor yet be rejected? Your seal is *well* known, and Your creatures are known by it. Your myriads have it; and in it the bachar-malachim are clothed.

---

[11] Bacharim = chosen ones; the elect. Bachar malachim = chosen messengers.

[12] El Shaddai = "The most high Elohim." Shaddai may also refer to the feminine characteristic of the Almighty to nurture and nourish. In the place of El Shaddai, we might employ El Elyon just as well.

[13] Yachad, yahad, echad = the mystical union spoken of in the shema on the high priestly prayer of John 17. The oneness of the like-minded.

[14] Ruach = spirit, wind, breath.

[15] Eli (ail-EE) = my Strong One, Psalms 22, etc.

[16] Tzadikim = those who believe and keep the commandments; those of justice.

You have given us Your fellowship; not that You were in need of us, but that we are ever in need of You. Sprinkle Your gentle sprinklings upon us and open Your prolific springs that supply us with milk and honey in abundance. You have no regrets (and even if You should regret anything You promised), since the ends were apparent to You beforehand.

What You gave, You freely gave. You will no longer draw them back or take them up again. For as Elohim, all was apparent to You and was set in order before You from the very beginning. And You, O MarYah, have made it all. Halleluyah.

5. **Love** [17]

I praise You, O MarYah, because I love You. El Shaddai, do not forsake me, for You are my hope! I received Your favor freely; now let me live by it.

My persecutors will surely come. Let them not see me! Let a cloud of darkness fall on their eyes; let a haze of thick darkness hide them! Let them have no light to see so they cannot seize me. Let their designs become vain so whatever they have conspired will return upon their own heads. For they have devised a plan that was not for them. They prepared themselves in cruelty, but they were discovered to be powerless.

Yea, my assurance is in MarYah. I will not fear. No, I will not fear for MarYah is El Yeshuati.[18] He is as a woven crown on my head, and I will not be shaken. Even if everything is shaken, I will stand firm. And even though all things visible should perish, I will not die; for MarYah is with me, and I am with Him. Halleluyah.

6. **Wind**

As the wind glides across the harp and the strings speak, the Ruach of MarYah speaks through my members, and I speak through His love. For He shatters whatever is not-of-me so that

---

[17] This entire ode is attributed to 'Salome' in the *Pistis Sophia* 58:9.

[18] Yeshuati = my yeshua, my rescuer.

everything is of Him. This is how it has been from the start, and will be until the end. So that nothing will deviate, and nothing will rise up against Him.

MarYah has multiplied his knowledge; He has been zealous to make known all that His favor has granted us. He gave us His name to praise, and our ruachim praise His Ruach haQodesh.[19]

A stream went forth and became a great and broad river; in fact, it carried them all away, crushing them and bringing them to the Temple. The barriers built by men were not able to hold it back; nor the craft of those who always hold back water. Yes, it spread over the surface of the entire world and filled all. Then all the thirsty in the world drank; thirst was quenched; *the thirsty* relieved; for El Shaddai provided the draught.

Great are those who serve the drink; all those who have been entrusted with His water. They have refreshed the parched lips, and aroused the paralyzed will. Even the living who were about to expire have been held back from death. Shattered limbs have they set and restored. They gave strength for their future and light for their eyes. Everyone recognized these waters as MarYah's own, and they remained beside the living water of eternity. Halleluyah.

7. **Pathway**

As anger makes its pathway over the Lawless, so is joy's pathway over the Beloved: it harvests its fruits without hindrance. My joy is in MarYah, and my course is set toward Him; my pathway is beautiful! Indeed, there is a Helper for me – it is MarYah. He has generously shown Himself to me in His simplicity, for His kindness has diminished His dreadfulness.

He became like me so I could receive Him. He was measured like me in form so that I could wear Him. I did not tremble when I saw Him because He was courteous to me. His nature became like mine so I might comprehend Him. His figure became like mine so I might not turn away from Him.

---

[19] Qodesh, Qadosh = set-apart, devoted, holy.

The Father of knowledge is the Word of knowledge. He who created wisdom is wiser than His works. He created me when I knew not yet what I should do when I came into being. On account of this, He favored me in His rich charity. He allowed me to question Him and benefit from His sacrifice. He is incorruptible. He is the completion of the worlds; and he is their Father.

He has allowed Himself to appear to His own so they may identify Him *as the One* who made them, and not assume they came of themselves. He has set His path on the way to knowledge; he widened it and lengthened it and brought it to total completion. Over it, He suspended traces of His light. I walked there – from beginning to end. These things have come forth from Him as He was resting in the Son. And He will hold everything *together* by His saving acts.

El Shaddai will be known by Her Qadoshim; those who have songs to announce MarYah's coming; those going out to meet Him, singing to Him with joy, and playing the harp of many notes.[20] *Yea*, the Seers will go before Him, and before Him they will be seen. They will praise MarYah in His love because He is near - and He does see! Hatred will be removed from the world along with jealousy – it will be drowned. Ignorance was destroyed in upon the arrival of MarYah's Knowledge.

Let the singers sing about the favor of MarYah El Shaddai, and let them bring out their songs. Let their hearts be like the day; their gentle voices like MarYah's majestic beauty. Let no one who breathes be without knowledge or voice. For He gave a mouth to His creation: to open the mouth's voice to Him, and to praise Him; to confess His power and declare His favor. Halleluyah.

---

[20] The title Shaddai may have a feminine connotation, according to mainstream scholars. Qadoshim – those who have devoted themselves from the world to the Eternal – set-apart or holy ones.

8. **Excitement**

Open, open your hearts to the excitement of MarYah, and let your love abound from the heart to the lips. Bring forth fruits for MarYah – a devoted life –speaking in His light with care.

Rise up and stand straight, you who were sometimes brought low. And you who were in silence, speak out; for your mouth has been opened! You who were despised – from now-on be lifted, for your righteousness has been lifted! Indeed, MarYah's right hand is with you, and He will be your Helper! Shalom has been prepared for you, going before *you in* what could have been your battle!

Hear the word of truth and receive the knowledge of El Shaddai! Your body may not understand what I am about to tell you; your clothing may not understand what I am about to show you. Keep My mystery, you who are kept by it! Keep My faith, you who are reserved by it! Understand My knowledge, you who know Me in truth! Love Me with affection, you who love!

I do not turn My face from My own; I know them! Even before they existed, I recognized them and imprinted a seal upon their faces. I fashioned their members, and My own breasts I prepared for them so they might drink My blessed milk and live by it.

I am pleased by them and am not ashamed of them; for they are My workmanship and the power of My ideas. Who is able to stand against My work? Or who is not subject to it? I willed then fashioned mind and heart, and they are My own. I have placed My Bacharim[21] on My right hand. My righteousness goes before them and they will not be deprived of My name, for it is with them.

Pray and increase, and abide in the love of MarYah, all you who are loved in the Beloved – all you who are kept in Him who lives – all you who are saved in Him who saves. You will be found uncorrupted throughout all ages on account of the name of your Father. Halleluyah.

---

[21] Bacharim – those whom I have chosen; the elect.

9. **Ears**

Open your ears and I will speak to you. Give yourself to Me so that I may give Myself back to you – even the word of MarYah and what He wants – even the pure idea He has thought concerning His Anointed. For your life is in the will of MarYah. His purpose is eternal life as your perfection is indestructible.

Be enriched in Elohim the Father and receive the purpose of El Shaddai for you. Be strong and redeemed by His favor. For I announce to you Qadoshim His shalom[22] so that none of those who hear will fall in battle – so that those who have known Him may not perish – so that those who received Him may not be ashamed.

Truth is an everlasting crown; blessed are the ones who plait it upon their heads. It is *like* precious stone; for the battles were on account of the crown! But Righteousness has taken it away *from them* and given it to you. Don the crown in MarYah's true covenant, and all those who have conquered will be inscribed in His book. For the book is the reward of your victory. She sees you there before her and wills you to be rescued. Halleluyah.

10. **Lips**

MarYah directed My lips with His Word and opened My heart with His Light. He made His abundant life to dwell within Me; He allowed Me to announce the fruit of His shalom to change the lives of all who want to come to Him, even as those who are caged up *want to come* to freedom.

I took courage and became strong. I captured the world; *I owned* its capture for the sake of the Shekinah of El Shaddai Elohim Avi.[23] The dispersed tribes were gathered in; I was not tainted by My love for them (though they praised Me in high places). Light-sparks *showered* their hearts; they walked in yachad with My life and were rescued. They became My people in timelessness. Halleluyah.

---

[22] Qadoshim .. shalom – those set apart unto Him, by His choosing or theirs .. peace or rest.

[23] Elohim Avi – My Father, the Strong One.

11. **Fruit**

My heart was pruned and its flower appeared, then favor sprang up within it. My heart made fruits for MarYah. El Shaddai circumcised me by His Ruach haQodesh before He uncovered my inward being, filled me with His love, and *pointed me* Him-ward. His circumcision became my Salvation; so I dashed into the Way, into His shalom, into the pathway of truth.[24] From beginning to end I received His knowledge.

Thus I was founded upon the Rock of Truth, where He set me down. Speaking waters from MarYah's fountain touched my lips in great measure. I drank to intoxication from the living water that never dies. My intoxication did not cause ignorance; no, I abandoned vanity, and turned *instead* toward Shaddai Eli. I was enriched by His favors. I rejected the vanity cast on the earth. I tore it away and cast it from me.

MarYah renewed me with His clothing; He possessed me by His light. From above He gave me everlasting Shabbat; I became like the land that blossoms and rejoices in its fruits. MarYah is like the sun on the face of the ground. My eyes were enlightened; my face received the dew; my breath was refreshed by the pleasant fragrance of MarYah.

He took me to His Gan Eden; the wealth of MarYah's pleasure there *dwells*. I beheld blooming and fruit-bearing trees, and their crown was self-grown. Their branches were sprouting; their fruits were glistening. An immortal land was within their roots. A river of gladness was irrigating them, rushing around them in the country of eternal life.

Then I worshipped MarYah for His magnificence. I said, Rab, O Yah, are those who are planted in Your land: who have a place in Your Eden, who grow within the span of Your trees, who have passed from darkness into light. Hinneh! All Your laborers are righteous; they do mitzvot tov.[25] They turn from cruelty to your friendliness. Yea, the heady perfume of Your trees is changing the land. Everyone here has become of remnant of

---

[24] My Salvation = Yeshuati.

[25] Mitzvot tov = good deeds. Or, "For the fragrant odor of trees changes in Your land."

You. So blesséd are the Your water-workers – Your faithful servants are timeless memorials.

Indeed, there is plenty of space in Your Eden. Nothing within is barren; everything is filled with fruit. May Esteem be Yours, O Elohim, in the delight of Pardes forever. Halleluyah.

12. **Words**

He has filled me with words of truth so that I may proclaim Him. Like flowing waters, truth flows from my mouth so my lips may declare His fruits. He caused His knowledge to thrive in me; for MarYah's lips are the true Word and door to His Light.

El Shaddai has given Him to His families – The interpreters of His beauty; The narrators of His radiance; The confessors of His reason; The preachers of His mind; The teachers of His works.

For the Word's subtlety is inexpressible. Like His utterance, so also is His swiftness and intensity; limitless is His progress. He never falls, but remains standing; one cannot comprehend His origin or His direction.[26] For as is *the expanse of* His work, so is His expectation; He is the light and dawning of thought.

By Him the families spoke to one another; those who were silent found *their* voice. Love and equality come from Him. *Families* spoke one to another of what was theirs. They were inspired by the Word, and knew Him who made them, because they were in harmony. For the lips of El Shaddai spoke to them; His exposition prospered through Him.

The dwelling place of the Word is Echad; His truth is love. Blesséd are those who (by Him) have perceived it all; those who have known MarYah in His truth. Halleluyah.

13. **Mirror**

Hinneh! MarYah is our mirror. Open your eyes to Him and see! Learn about your face then proclaim praises to His Ruach.

---

[26] Or, "His descent or His way."

Wipe your face of paint, love His devotion, and put it on instead. Then you will be flawless in Him always. Halleluyah.

14. **Eyes**

As the eyes of a son *look* upon his father, so are my eyes, O Yah, turned You-ward at all times. My breasts and my delight are with You. Do not turn your mercies away from me, O Yah; do not remove Your kindnesses from me. Stretch out Your right hand to me always, Sovereign. By Your will, be my guide until the *very* end.

Let me be pleasing to You in accordance to Your fame and Your name. Save me from the Evil One; allow Your gentility and the fruits of your love linger with me, O Yah. Teach me the odes of Your truth so I am able to render fruits in You. Play the harp of Your Ruach haQodesh for me; with every note I can praise You, O Yah. In your multitude of mercies, grant me these *requests*; yes! Hurry to grant our requests, since You*rs* are enough *to fulfill* all our needs. Halleluyah.

15. **Sun**

As the sun delights the seekers of its daybreak, so is my delight in MarYah. He is my sun! His rays raised me. His light bars all darkness from my face. I received *my* eyes from Him! I have seen His Yom Tov! He gave me ears, and I heard His truth! I accepted His wise ideas! In Him have I delighted fully.

I renounced the wrong way. Instead, I went Him-ward and from Him, I received a great salvation! He gave generously to me. He formed me in his excelling beauty. By His name, I put on timeless life; and by His favor, I and took off corruption. For my future, death is destroyed; by my word, Sheol is defeated. In MarYah's nation, timelessness arises! Life is proclaimed for His Enumin.[27] Unlimited life is granted to all who trust in Him. Halleluyah.

---

[27] Emunim = His faithful.

16. **Singing**

Just as the plowman's work is the plow and the helmsman's work the helm, so also my work is MarYah's tehillah –His odes.[28] My craft and service are His odes, for His love has nourished my heart, and He poured His fruits on my lips. MarYah is my love; I will sing to Him. His praises strengthen me; I have *complete* faith in Him.

I will open my mouth and MarYah's Ruach will speak of His favor and beauty through me: the work of His hands; the labor of His fingers; the host of His mercies; the strength of His Word. For the Miltha-MarYah[29] investigates the invisible, illuminating His ideas. The eye spies His works while the ear hears His thoughts.

MarYah Himself made a wide earth and positioned the waters in the sea. He expanded the sky and attached the stars. He fixed the creation; *He* set it up then rested from His works. Now creatures run in their courses. They do what they were meant to do; they can never quit or fail. The myriads are subject to His Miltha.

The sun is the reservoir of light and the moon is the reservoir of dark. He made the sun for the daylight's light; but the night convey darkness over the face of the earth. All these[30] pieces, one after another, complete the beauty of Elohim.

Outside of MarYah is nothing; He exists before anything came to be. The worlds are by His Miltha, even by His heart's thought. Praise and honor *are due* His name. Halleluyah.

17. **Freedom**

Once Eli crowned me, and My crown was alive.[31] Once I was vindicated by My Master, and My salvation *became* undying. I am free from self and condemned no longer. His hands spliced

---

[28] Tehillah = Song or psalm.

[29] Miltha = Ar. Word.

[30] Or, "all their pieces."

[31] "Once," or "Then." Eli, pronounced ail'EE, meaning "my Elohim."

My chains. I received the face and air of the New Man. I walked in Him and was saved.

Thoughts of truth led Me. I went after *them*; I did not stray. All who saw Me were amazed, for I seemed a stranger to them. But El Shaddai in all His perfection was He who knew Me and dignified Me. He esteemed Me highly in His kindness and raised My comprehension to the full height of truth. From there He gave me the map[32] of His own footsteps.

I opened closed doors. I shattered bars of iron. My own shackles heated then melted before me. Nothing appeared closed to Me. *Yea*, I was opening everything. By my own choice, I went to free all the hostages, not wanting to leave anyone chained up behind.

I circulated My knowledge generously, even My rising, on account of My love.[33] I sowed My fruits to hearts, transforming them through Me. They received My blessing and lived. They were gathered into Me and rescued. They became My limbs and I their Head. Great honor be Yours, our Head, O MarYah. Halleluyah.

18. **Heart**

My heart was lifted up and enriched in the love of El Shaddai, so that I might praise Him with My name.[34] My limbs were strengthened, so they may not fall away from His power. Infirmities fled my body. I stood firm for MarYah (as is His desire), because His reign is firmly *established.*

O Yah, for the sake of those who are in need, do not dismiss Your Word from Me, nor, for the sake of their works, withhold Your perfection from Me. Let not light be beaten by darkness, nor let truth be scattered from falsehood. Allow Your right hand to set our salvation for *complete* victory from every locale. Hold it tight for the sake of all beset by trouble.

---

32 Or, "pathway."

33 Rising, or "Resurrection."

34 If this is the Nazorean speaking, we understand that his name, Yahshua, reflects the name of the Almighty, MarYah, Yahweh.

You are Eli; Your lips *speak* neither falsehood or death – You desire only perfection. There is nothing that You do not know, since 'Nothing' knows you not! You know no error, since 'Error' knows you not! 'Ignorance' came like dust or sea scum. The Useless think 'Ignorance is Strength'; they became his sort and were thereby impoverished.

But those in the know understand by logic and remained unpolluted by their notions. Such were in the mind of El Shaddai, who scorns those walking in 'Error.' But *the Perfect* speak truth by El Shaddai's breath breathing in them; praise and great honor to His name! Halleluyah.

19. **Milk**

A cup of milk was offered me. I drank it in the sweetness of MarYah's kindness. The Son is the cup and the Father is He who was milked. The Ruach haQodesh is She who milked. Why? Because His breasts were full, and it was wrong that His milk should be wasted.

The Ruach haQodesh opened Her bosom and mixed the milk of the Father's breasts. She gave the mix to the family without their knowing. Even so, the ones who received milk are in the perfection of the right hand.

The womb of the Virgin received it, and she conceived and gave birth. So the Virgin became a mother of great compassion. She labored and bore the Son –without pain, but not without purpose. She needed no midwife; He caused her to speak life!

Willfully, she birthed, bearing according to the sign, received of El Elyon. She loved with liberation; protected with placidly; declared with dignity. Halleluyah.

20. **Priest**

I am Maryah's priest; I serve Him as a priest. I offer Him a gift of His own thought. He doesn't think like those of the world; neither like those of flesh or those who worship the flesh. Virtue and purity of heart and lips are *proper* gifts for Him.

Offer your faultless inward being! Do not allow sympathy to repress your compassion, nor your self to repress *your* soul. You should not buy a stranger because he is like you, nor try to deceive your neighbor, nor deprive him of his clothing (that he be naked). Put on MarYah's favor liberally instead.

Come into His Eden and make yourself a wreath from His tree. Put it on your head and be joyful. Recline during His Shabbat; His Shekinah will go before you and you will receive a part of His kindness and favor. You will be anointed in the truth, with the praise of His virtue. Praise and honor His name! Halleluyah.

21. **Arms**

I lifted my arms high *toward* MarYah's love. I did so because He cast off My chains; *yes*, *through* His compassion and salvation, My Helper lifted me! I put off darkness and put on light. I received new parts! In them there was no sickness, affliction, or suffering.

Thinking of MarYah and His timeless fellowship helped Me greatly. I was lifted into the light as I passed before Him. While praising and confessing Him, I was near Him constantly.

He caused my heart to overflow; I found My heart in My mouth, springing forth to my lips. MarYah's excitement and praise increased all the more on my face. Halleluyah.

22. **Hand**

He who caused My descent from high up and ascent from regions below – He who gathers things between and casts them to Me – He who scattered My enemies and My adversaries – He who gave Me authority over bondage to unchain them – He who overthrew the seven-headed dragon with My hands and set Me at its roots so I might destroy its seed[35] – You were there! You *did* help Me! You were everywhere! Your name surrounded Me!

---

[35] Revelation 12:3.

Your right hand destroyed his poisoned[36] venom; yea, Your hand leveled the road before those who believe in You. From tombs Your hand chose them and separated them from the dead. *Your hand* took the dead bones and covered them with flesh. They did not move, so *Your hand* rendered them the energy to live. Your way and Your face are imperishable. You destroyed Your world so all things might be resolved and renewed.

Your rock is the foundation of all things. On it You built Your nation, which became the habitation of the qadoshim. Halleluyah.

23. **Finger**

Joy is for the Qadoshim. Who would be able to put on *such joy* but these alone? Favor is for the Bacharim. Who would be able to receive *such favor* but those who trusted from the first? Love is for the Qadoshim. Who would be able to put on such love but those who had it from the beginning?

Walk in MarYah's knowledge, and you will receive MarYah's generous favor for both His praise and the perfection of His knowledge.

His thought was like a letter descending by his wish from high above. It was sent out forcefully – like an arrow from a bow. Many hands hurried to catch the message – to take it and read it – but it escaped their fingers.

They were afraid of it and its seal since they were not permitted to loosen its seal. The seal's power was greater than them all. Yet those who saw the letter *fall* went after it to discover its landing place and who would read and hear it.

But a wheel received it and rolled over it. A sign was on it, *the sign* of the reign and of destiny. Whatever disturbed the wheel, it mowed down. It held back multitudes of shatanim.[37] It bridged rivers. It rolled over many forests, uprooting *trees*,

---

[36] Or, "evil."

[37] Or, "adversaries."

creating open road. When the wheel ran over the bottom of something, the rest of it was *pulled in and destroyed*, even to the top, and whatever else it came upon.

The letter contained commandments; all *political* regions were gathered together for it. At the beginning of the letter, the Head was revealed – haBen-Emet Av l'El Shaddai.[38] He inherited everything! and he took it all! So then, the devious plotting of many came to an end. Seducers, intractable *in their sin*, fled away; all tormenters were stomped out to extinction.

The letter became a great volume, written entirely by The Finger of Elohim. The Father's Name signed it; and the Name of the Son of the Ruach haQodesh was *designated* to rule without end. Halleluyah.

24. **Dove**

The dove fluttered over our Sovereign Messiah's head, as He was Her head.[39] She sang above Him, and Her voice was heard. Those who lived around there were scared; even the strangers were troubled. The bird began to fly, and every creeping thing died in its lair.[40] The chasms were opened and closed; one and all were seeking MarYah as if they were about to give birth. Yet He was not given to them to sustain them, because He did not belong to them.

Those of the chasms were all drowned in MarYah's seal; they perished on account of the *puerile* notions they had held *as truth* from the start. They were all in labor from the beginning; the end of their travail was life. All those *found* wanting perished, because they could not express the *appropriate* word to remain *instead.*

MarYah destroyed the devices of those who no truth within them. They lacked wisdom so they puffed themselves up in their

---

[38] Ben Emet ... = "Father El Shaddai the Mighty's Son of Truth."

[39] Matthew 3:16, Mark 1:10, Luke 3:22, John 1:32. We see an evolution of the dove, beginning as a metaphor of the Ruach haQodesh, to an actual dove resting upon Him, and now the dove is singing. These passages compared make for a very revealing study.

[40] Or, "hole."

mind. Thus they were rejected – the truth was not in them. But MarYah revealed His way; He spread his favor widely. And those who understood it came to know His sanctity[41] as well. Halleluyah.

25. **Rescue**

When I was rescued[42] from my chains, I fled to You, O Eli; for You are Salvation's right hand and my Advocate.[43] You held back those who rose against me: they are no longer seen. Your face was with me; it saved me by Your favor.

I was despised and rejected in the eyes of many. In their eyes, I was as heavy as lead. But from You I received my strength and help. You set a lamp for me – one on my right and another on my left – so nothing but light might surround me. I was covered with Your Ruach's cover; so I removed my clothing of skin.

Because Your right hand held me up, sickness passed away from me. I became chason in Your 'emet and qodesh in Your tzedekah.[44] All my enemies were afraid of me when, by the name of Yahweh, I became MarYah's *possession*. In his kindness, I was acquitted. His Shabbat is timeless. Halleluyah.

26. **Odes**

I poured out praise to MarYah, for I am His. I will recite His devoted ode; my heart is with Him. My hand holds His harp; His odes of Shabbat cannot be silenced. I will call to Him with all my heart; I will praise and raise Him with all my parts. His praise is from East to West; from South to North *rings* His thanksgiving. His perfection exists from the apex of *each* summit and outward to their extremities.

---

[41] Or, "holiness," "devotion," or "oneness."

[42] "Rescue," "salvation," "saved," and "help" all define Yahshua / Yeshua.

[43] Or, "You are the right hand of salvation, and my Helper / Paraclete."

[44] Chason = strong; 'emet = truth; qodesh = set-apart; tzedekah = Torah-doing.

Who is able to write the odes of MarYah, or even read them? Who can train for *such a* life so he may be saved? Or who is able to press in upon El Shaddai, so as to recite from His very lips?

Who can interpret the wonders of MarYah? Such a one will perish, yet the interpretation will remain. That *alone* is enough to identify and be satisfied –as the odists perform[45] in serenity – even as the spring gushes *crescendo* in the river. Such water flows to relieve all who seek it out. Halleluyah.

27. **Tree**

I extended my hands, paying homage to my Sovereign, for His sign is my outstretched arms,[46] and my expanse is the upright tree. Halleluyah.

28. **Wings**

As the doves' wings protect their nestlings and the nestlings' mouths are near the doves' mouths, so also are the wings of the Ruach protecting my heart. Yea, my heart revives itself continually! It leaps for joy *within me* as a babe leaps in her mother's womb.

I trusted, and I was at rest; for trustworthy is He in whom I trusted. He has greatly blessed me, and my mind[47] is with Him. The dagger will not divide me from Him, neither will the sword; I am well prepared before destruction arrives. I am positioned on His immortal side. Undying Life embraced me and kissed me. That kind of life is from the Ruach, who dwells within me. It cannot die since it is Life!

Those who saw me were dismayed; and I was persecuted *accordingly*. They thought I was swallowed up. I seemed to them as one of the lost. The injustice *I received* became my salvation. (I had become a scandal among them, because in me was no jealousy.)

---

[45] That is, the standing up.

[46] Or, "hands."

[47] Or, "head."

Yes, because I always did good to every one *of them*, I was hated. They surrounded me like mad dogs; like dogs that stupidly attack their masters. Their thinking is depraved; their minds, perverted.

My right hand was toting water while enduring their bitterness by my sweetness.[48] I did not perish, for I was neither their kin nor was my birth like theirs. They sought my death, but found that impossible; for I was older than their memory. They cast dice against me for naught. Those set against me tried vainly to destroy the memory of the One who was before them. El Shaddai's way of thinking cannot be captured. His heart is above and beyond all wisdom. Halleluyah.

29. **Hope**

MarYah is my hope; I will not be ashamed of Him. By His praise He made me. By His favor He provisioned me. By His mercy He honored me. By His great honor He lifted me. He made me to rise from Sheol's lowest pit. He pulled me out of Death's mouth. I humbled my enemies *when*, by His favor, He vindicated me *fully*.

I believed in MarYah's Anointed One, and thought, "He *too* is MarYah!" So He revealed His sign to me. He led me by His light. He gave me His power-rod so that I might check the people's devices and humiliate the powerful. By His Word I make war; I seize the victory by His power.

Yea, by His Word MarYah deposed my enemy like dust in the wind. I gave praise to El Shaddai! He made His servant great, even the son of His maidservant. Halleluyah.

30. **Fountain**

Fill yourselves with water from MarYah's living fountain! It is open to you! Come all you thirsty and take a drink! Rest beside MarYah's sparkling fountain; it is so pleasant. It refreshes the soul every time. Its water is much sweeter than the

---

[48] Maror .. matuki = "I endured their bitterness by my sweetness."

others;[49] even a honeycomb cannot compare. Why? It flows from the MarYah's lips; and from His heart it is named. It came *to them* boundlessly, but invisibly; yet until it was set in *their very* midst, they did not recognize it. Blessed are the ones who have drunk from it, and been refreshed by it. Halleluyah.

Response:

30a. **Drink**

Drink, drink deeply – the living fountain of
    your friend is yours. It is yours.
Come, you thirsty and rest beside the fountain of
    your friend. It is yours.
How beautiful and pure, how quenching to the thirst!
Drink deeply from the fountain of Messiah!

Drink, drink deeply – the water of the fountain
    is so sweet. Honey sweet.
Come, you thirsty; the combs of bees have nothing
    to compare, and it's yours.
It flows down from the lips of the Almighty One.
Its name is from the heart of your Messiah.

Come, you thirsty to rest beside the fountain
    of your friend. It is yours.
Drink, drink deeply, for those who drink are blessed
    and they rest; O, they rest.
Their thirst is satisfied in his e'er-bubbling spring.
They rest deep in the bosom of Messiah!

31. **Chasms**

Chasms vanished before MarYah's presence; darkness dissipated. Error erred and expired on His account. No inroad was given Contempt; he was drowned in MarYah's truth.

Mari opened His mouth, speaking favor and joy, rehearsing a new ode to His name. He lifted his voice, offering to El Shaddai those who had become sons through Him. His

---

[49] Or, "many."

countenance was vindicated *as though by a* gift of His Av ha Qodesh.

Come forth, you who have been afflicted, and receive joy! Own your souls by *His* favor; take timeless life to yourselves!

They condemned me when I stood up; I had not previously been condemned. They split up my stuff, though nothing was owed them. I survived – I held my peace and was silent, so they might not *further* agitate me.

I stood like solid rock constantly pounded by high columns of waves. I endured *it all*. By humility, I held up under their bitterness. I wanted to teach my tribe and convert it lest I nullify *my* pledge to our ancestors. My promise? *To be there* for the salvation of *all* their descendents. Halleluyah.

32. **Power**

About the Baruchim – joy *springs* from their hearts as light from the One who lives within: He is the Miltha h'emet, the self-originated Echad, edified by the power reserve of the El Elyon.[50] This is why He is unshakable, and for all time. Halleluyah.

33. **Virgin**

Yet again Favor rapidly expelled the Corruptor, descending over him, renouncing him. For *the Corruptor* obliterated everything that was in front of him; all his works were corrupt.

He stood on a summit's highest peak and cried out to all the ends of the earth. He drew to himself all who would obey him; for he did not seem to be the Evil One *to them*.

All the while, the Perfect Virgin was standing by, proclaiming and beckoning: O you Bnei-Adam, Shuv! You their daughters, Nu Kvar![51] Abandon the Corruptor's ways! Come to me!

---

[50] Baruchim = the blessed ones; Miltha h'emet = the Word of Truth; Echad = the One; reserved = set-apart, 'holy'; El Elyon = the Most High Power.

[51] Bnei-Adam = sons of adam; shuv = turn around, repent! Nu Kvar = come forth!

I will come among you to bring you out from destruction to teach you ways of truth. Do not become corrupt nor perish! Obey me and be saved, for I declare Elohim's favor to you! By me you will be rescued and blessed. Am I not your judge?

Those who have clothed themselves with me will not be falsely accused; no! The freshness of the new world is theirs! My Bacharim are walking with me; yet I will make my paths known to any who will seek me. I promise them my Name. Halleluyah.

34. **Image**

There is no rough road for the simple-hearted; no fence for righteous thoughts; no whirlwind in the deep recesses of an enlightened idea; no inner division in the one surrounded by pleasant country on all sides.

The image of the above is the reality of the below. All things come from above. From below there is nothing – except what is perceived by those of no understanding.

Great favor has been revealed to you for salvation. Believe, live, be saved! Halleluyah.

35. **Showers**

MarYah's gentle showers shaded me in serenity; they made the shalom-cloud rise above my head, guarding me forever. It became Yeshuati.[52] Everyone *else* was upset and afraid; from them came the smoke of judgment. But I was calm in the midst of MarYah's host; he was more than my shade; yea! far more than foundation! For I was carried like a child by its mother. He gave me milk: the dew of MarYah. I was nourished by His favor. I rested in His perfection.

I spread out my arms in my ascent, directing myself towards El Shaddai, and I was transforming[53] *even as I sped* toward Him. Halleluyah.

---

[52] Yeshuati = my salvation; my Yahshua.

[53] Or, "redeeming."

36. **Spirit**

I rested on MarYah's Ruach, and She lifted me up into the sky. She made me stand on my feet in MarYah's high place, before His perfection and His kavod, where I continually venerated Him by composing His Odes.

The Ruach brought me before MarYah's face; and because I was the Ben Adam, named for the Light, the Ben Elohim; the most celebrated among the kavodim, the greatest among the rabbim.[54]

For She made me in proportion to El Shaddai's importance; then in proportion to His newness, He renewed me.

He anointed me with His perfection; I came to be among those who are near Him. My mouth was opened like a dew-cloud; my heart surged like a surge of righteousness. I drew nearer in shalom; I was established in the destiny's ruach. Halleluyah.

37. **Rest**

I stretched out my hands to MarYah; I raised my voice to El Shaddai. I spoke out with the lips of my heart. When my voice reached Him, He listened. Then His Word came to me, to grant me my labor's fruits. By His favor, MarYah gave me shalom. Halleluyah.

Response:

37a. **Stretch**

I stretch out my hands, to you! My being is parched for you!
Teach me the way to go; preach me the mind to know;
Fetch me the seeds to sow into this arid land!

Hasten to speak to me; chasten and set me free:
In you, O Yah, I put my trust, to you I lift up my soul.

Deliver me! O set me free!
Let your clean Ruach lead me to higher ground!
Recover me! O let me be,

---

[54] Kavodim = the famous ones; rabbim = the great ones.

Like your dear Son, I stretch my hands.
To heaven's silent sounds, I stretch my hands.

38. **Truth**

I rode up into the light of Truth as though in a chariot.[55] Truth led me *upward*, drawing me nearer. He made me pass over chasms and gulfs, saving me from cliffs and valleys. He became a sanctuary of salvation to me; He set me *down* on the plateau of timeless life.[56]

He went with me, making me rest, yet not allowing me to err; for He was and is the Truth. I was not in danger, because I was walking with Him consistently. No, I did not make a single wrong move, because I obeyed Him. Error fled away from Him, never meeting Him *at all*.

Truth preceded *me* on the upright way; whatever I did not understand He showed me, like all the poisons of error and pains of death (that some think sweet). I saw the Corruptor corrupting: yea, the depraved bride all festooned[57] with the degenerate groom who corrupts *her*.

I asked Truth, Who are they? He told me: They are the Deceiver and the Error. They imitate the Beloved and His Bride, causing the world to err *in its imitation*, thus corrupting it all. They invite many to the*ir* reception, letting all drink the drugged wine until they regurgitate[58] their wisdom and knowledge to prepare them for stupidity. Then their *hosts* abandon them; so they stumble around in madness and corruption. Since they have lost their minds, they no longer seek out understanding.

But I have been warned not to fall into the hands of the Deceivers. I rejoiced because the Truth accompanied me. I was well-grounded, and I lived *to be* redeemed. My foundations were laid by the plan of MarYah's hand; He planted me. He set the

---

55 Chariot = merkavah (RKB).

56 Plateau = locale or plane – a flat landing area.

57 Or, "adorned," "decked out."

58 Regurgitate = puke; throw up as the drunken often do.

root; He watered it and endowed it and blessed it, and its fruits are timeless.

The roots broke through and reached their depth. The *branch* sprang up and spread out, becoming high and full. MarYah alone was praised in His planting and gardening, in His caring and in the blessing of His lips, in the beautiful sowing of His right hand, in the success of His farming, and in His mind's fond thoughts. Halleluyah.

39. **Rivers**

The power of MarYah is the rage of rivers; He sends those who despise Him head over heels; tangling up their paths, tearing out their roots; snatching away their bodies; wrecking their lives.

His rivers are faster than lightning; yea, even faster than that. But those who walk over *His rivers* in trust will not be afraid. Those who walk upon them perfectly will not even be stressed. *Why not?* MarYah's sign is upon them; that sign is the Way for those who walk in the name of MarYah.

Therefore, put on the name of El Elyon and get to know Him; then you will walk without danger since rivers will obey you. MarYah, by His Word, has bridged them, crossing them on foot. His steps stand firm upon the waters without ruin; indeed, they are like a beam of wood built upon *a foundation of* truth.

The waves rose high on this side and that, but the feet of our Mar-MarYah stand firm.[59] They are neither washed away nor ruined. The Way has been paved[60] for those who step over after Him, for those who remain true to the path of His faith; also *for all those* who love His name. Halleluyah.

---

[59] Mar MarYah is an expression exactly like Yah Yahweh in Isaiah 12:2 "Behold El is my Salvation - I shall trust and not live in fear - for my strength and power is *Yah Yahweh*, becoming for me the *yahshua* (salvation)."

[60] Or, "chosen."

40. **Honey**

As honey drips from the bees' comb and milk flows from the woman who loves her children, so also *all* my hope is conveyed through You, Eli. As a fountain gushes forth its water, so my heart gushes forth with admiration for MarYah, and my lips carry forth praise to Him. His anthems sweeten my tongue; His odes anoint *all* my members.

My face rejoices in His jubilation; my ruach is lifted high in His love; my nephesh shines in Him. If the fearful will trust Him, redemption through Him is assured. His wealth is timeless life; those who receive it cannot perish. Halleluyah.

41. **Babes**

Let all MarYah's babes praise Him! May we all receive the truth of faith in Him! He knows all His children, so let us sing about His love!

By MarYah's favor, we live in Him. We receive life by His Anointed One. A great day has shined upon us; His Shekinah is awesome.[61] So in yachad, let us all agree in the name of Yahweh, and honor Him in His goodness.[62]

May our faces shine by His light! May our hearts think by His love! Night and day, may we all thrill and rejoice in Master Yahweh!

All those who see me will be stunned, for I am of a different race. The Father of Truth remembered me; the One who possessed me from the start. Indeed, His riches and His heart's idea conceived me.

His Word is with us in all our pathways; the Savior gives us life and never discards us. The Man who humbled Himself became famous by His righteousness.

---

[61] Shekinah (f.) = the living space of Yahweh; or, the radiance of that space, often translated 'glory.'

[62] Yachad or Yahad = in one accord, together.

Yea, the Ben El Shaddai appeared in the perfection of His Father. Light dawned from the Miltha,[63] from the beforetime within Him. In truth, the Anointed One is Echad.

Before the world's foundation, it was known already that He would give timeless life through the truth of His name. Halleluyah. (This new ode is dedicated to MarYah by the ones who love Him.)

Response:

41a. **Alien**

I am the alien among you;
I am from somewhere you can't see –
Far from here.
I pass through light; I pass through matter;
For the Father engender'd me to pass!

Pass on through the mountains and the vales of his heart;
He possess'd me from the start.
The Father of all truth remember'd me,
And that's why all the world –
Yes, that's why all the world –
That's why all the world is astonished, is astonished!
Aren't we astonished in the Light of the Son?

I may pass you back to life from death and I will.
I will not forget your souls!
For light and life found daybreak in my Word –
and I save souls in truth –
and save them in my name.
That's why all the world is astonished, is astonished!
Aren't we together in the life of the ONE?

The humble are exalted, aren't they?
One in Messiah; we're uplifted!
One in the body of Elohim!
And one is our love for Him!

---

63 Miltha = Aramaic, Word, Logos.

42. **Door**

I stretch out my hands, drawing near to Mari; for my stretched-out hands is His sign.[64] My reach is the standing tree, lifted high along the road of the Righteous One. I was of no use to those who did not hold me *up*; I will *rather* be with those who love me.

Now all my persecutors are dead: all those who hunted me, all who vetoed me, all because I was alive. Now I have risen and am with them. I will speak with their mouths, for they have loathed the ones who persecuted them.

So I lifted the burden of my love over them. Like the arm of the bridegroom around the bride, my yoke surrounds those who know me. Just as the bed is spread inside the chamber of the bride and groom, my love spreads over all those who believe me.

Although I was considered to be discarded, I was not. Although they thought I had perished, I did not. Indeed, Sheol saw me and was shattered, and Death debarred me and many with me. I have been vinegar and gall to Abaddon,[65] and I descended down as deep as it goes. He unlocked *my* head and feet; he could not endure my face.

I built a living congregation from his dead. I spoke with them all by living lips so my word might not be without value. Those who died ran towards me. They cried out, saying, Ben Elohim, take pity on us! Deal with us from Your kindness! Fetch us from the bonds of gloom. Open the door so we may come out to You (for we reckon our death does not touch You). May we also be rescued along with You! You are our Savior!

I heard their voices. I placed their assurance in my heart. I set My name upon their foreheads – for now they are free and they are mine.[66] Halleluyah.

---

[64] Mari = 'my Sovereign' or 'My Master.'

[65] The term Abaddon is the personification of Death and also the place of the dead. Abaddon means something like 'nothingness' or 'total destruction.'

[66] The name Y'shua (Jəsus) means "Yahweh's Rescuer."

Other Publications from this Author

Codex Sinaiticus: The H. T. Anderson New Testament – Anderson's famous and rare English translation (1866) of the 3rd to 4th century Sinaiticus Greek New Testament, thought by scholars to be the earliest complete New Testament manuscript in existence. This is a first edition of the text published in easy-to-read Georgia font with 2 points between verses. My publication also includes public domain versions of the last books of the Sinaiticus; that is, Epistle of Barnabas and Shepherd of Hermas. I also included the Didache, or Teaching of the Twelve, since it has such affinity with Barnabas. Please check out my new translation of Barnabas from the

I Enoch, Sky-tripper: First Enoch, True Names Version –Snyder's new edition of 1 Enoch takes into account Isaac's annotation on the Coptic translation, the English translations of Isaac and Laurence, and the latest editions of the Dead Sea Scroll portions. Technical terms are rendered in Hebrew transliteration, as are proper names and places. Excessive wordiness has been eliminated, updated definitions clarify ancient word meanings, and the errors of pre-1950 translations are corrected. Includes a glossary of Hebrew technical terms left untranslated in this edition.

The Nazarene Acts of he Apostles or The Recognitions of Clement– Ever wonder why Simon Peter only got a couple short letters in our Scriptures? Wouldn't someone have recorded Peter's AUTHENTIC acts and preaching? Of course his preaching was recorded! By Clement, an affluent Gentile convert, at the command of James the Just. So why would the Church Fathers bury the preaching of their first pope since Clement was their second pope? Because Peter's teachings are HEBRAIC. This volume is one-of-a-kind, containing teachings on many subjects, including deliverance, healing, true worship, and lost doctrines. We dispensed with churchy language and restored the original Hebraic names and titles of people, places and concepts - and a full glossary.

The Letter of Bar Naba's to His Spiritual Children: The Epistle of Barnabas – This volume includes the following unique features: a scholarly introduction, a brand new translation from the Greek with comparisons to the Hoole and Lightfoot translations, Interpaginated with the Revised Greek of the Ante Nicene Fathers, Over 150 annotations and Tanakh references, Essays explaining the "Teachings of the Three Letters" and "The Teachings of the Eight Days," Plenty of room for your personal notes. Explanations of several unique mysteries of the Bible and a few mysteries as yet unsolved.

***Kata Mattyah: According to Matthew* - A New Translation from Ancient Witnesses.** Translated from 3rd Century Sinaitic Manuscript א And Diligently Compared With The H. L. Anderson New Testament (begun in 1861), The Dead Sea Scrolls, The Aramaic Peshitta, and The Nestlé-Aland 26 Greek Text: For Readers of the English Language. Kata Mattyah is very useful for gaining a command of the biblical Hebrew language. Many common transliterated Hebrew words replace their English counterparts so that the student progressing through this version will gain a basic Hebrew vocabulary. Includes full text of Matthew, annotations, pronunciation guide, and complete Hebrew, Aramaic, Latin & Greek Glossary.

Spiritual Gifts Revelation: Miracles by the Book – If the New Covenant accurately contains the teaching of the Son of Elohim, then should not his followers also be able to accomplish his feats? If Yahshua "ever lives and ever loves," then should not his people be the personal extension of his astounding capabilities? There are many evidences that indeed Yahshua still works miracles, both small and great, and that he PREVENTS evil. Snyder thinks he can help show those willing how they may proceed. He takes us on a journey through Scripture and his own life to expose tiny miracles and exposit what kind of discipline in love is required to achieve them. This book is a hands-on Spiritual Gifts course for individuals or teams that can lead to certification in supernatural ministry.

Spiritual Gifts Revelation: Charismata, Theory, Assessment, Problem-solving – Most approaches to Motivational Gifts assessment lend themselves to faulty results due to a one-dimensional inventory strategy & conclusions based on lack of practice & data. Results are often inaccurate because survey answers are self-perceptions rather than actions. The Integrated Approach is multidimensional, including 5x3 dimensions of Temperament, thinking vs. doing exercises, & the 9-key Personality, to standard inventories. With help from 1000s of online participants, the author has found an "Integrated Approach"-a unique, accurate system that tears away the masks to the soul beneath. No longer mere Christian entertainment, the Rom 12 gifts render life-enhancing tools, helping participants analyze pathways accurately then make valid, prayerful decisions. This book is the first of a series. The 2nd covers Pneumatic and Apostolic Gifts. The 3rd, "Spiritual Restoration"; & the final volume brings the Integrated Approach all together.

EloHymnal – contains 102+ original manuscripted praise and worship songs written directly from the poetic passages of the Scriptures. These songs feature concepts from the Hebrew / Hebraic Roots of our faith. All are in English interspersed with important Hebraic terms. Many of the songs convey the Hebraic musical idiom or Klezmer style. Many are suitable for praise dancing. Fully orchestrated accompaniments free for the download.

www.ingramcontent.com/pod-product-compliance
Ingram Content Group UK Ltd.
Pitfield, Milton Keynes, MK11 3LW, UK
UKHW041902190726
13854UKWH00003B/1048